WEARING AN ARTIFICIAL LIMB

BY HARRIET BRUNDLE

HUMAN BODY HELPERS

BookLife PUBLISHING

©2019
BookLife Publishing Ltd.
King's Lynn
Norfolk PE30 4LS

All rights reserved.
Printed in Malaysia.

A catalogue record for this book is available from the British Library.

ISBN: 978-1-78637-715-9

Written by:
Harriet Brundle

Edited by:
John Wood

Designed by:
Danielle Jones

All facts, statistics, web addresses and URLs in this book were verified as valid and accurate at time of writing. No responsibility for any changes to external websites or references can be accepted by either the author or publisher.

The author of this book is not a medically trained professional. If you have any questions about artificial limbs, please see your doctor.

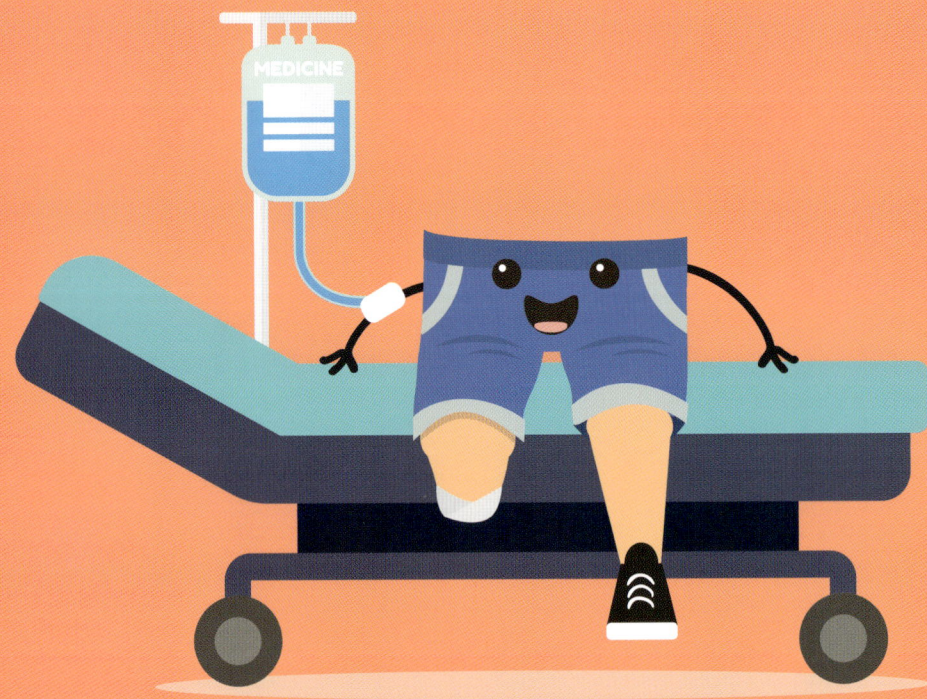

IMAGE CREDITS

All images are courtesy of Shutterstock.com, unless otherwise specified. With thanks to Getty Images, Thinkstock Photo and iStockphoto. Front Cover & 1 – grmarc, Beatriz Gascon J, NikaMooni, Milan M. Images used on every spread – grmarc, Beatriz Gascon J, NikaMooni, yana shypova. 20 – Elvetica, Inspiring, anitnov, Katy Flaty. 23 – Visual Generation.

CONTENTS

Page 4 — What are limbs?

Page 6 — What Is an Artificial Limb?

Page 8 — What Happens If I Need an Artificial Limb?

Page 14 — Getting an Artificial Limb

Page 16 — Wearing Your Artificial Limb

Page 20 — Dos and Don'ts

Page 22 — Life with Your Artificial Limb

Page 24 — Glossary and Index

Words that look like **this** can be found in the glossary on page 24.

WHAT ARE LIMBS?

Your limbs are your arms and legs.

Some people only have one of each, or none at all. They can be born this way, or could have had an illness or injury.

Hi, I'm Lee-Lee Legs and it's nice to meet you.

You may have a problem with one of your limbs or it hasn't grown in the way that it should. It could be that you have had to have a limb **removed** by having an **operation**.

WHAT IS AN ARTIFICIAL LIMB?

If you do not have two arms or two legs, it can be difficult to do some everyday things. This could mean that you need an **artificial** limb to make your life easier.

My name is Annie Artificial Limb.

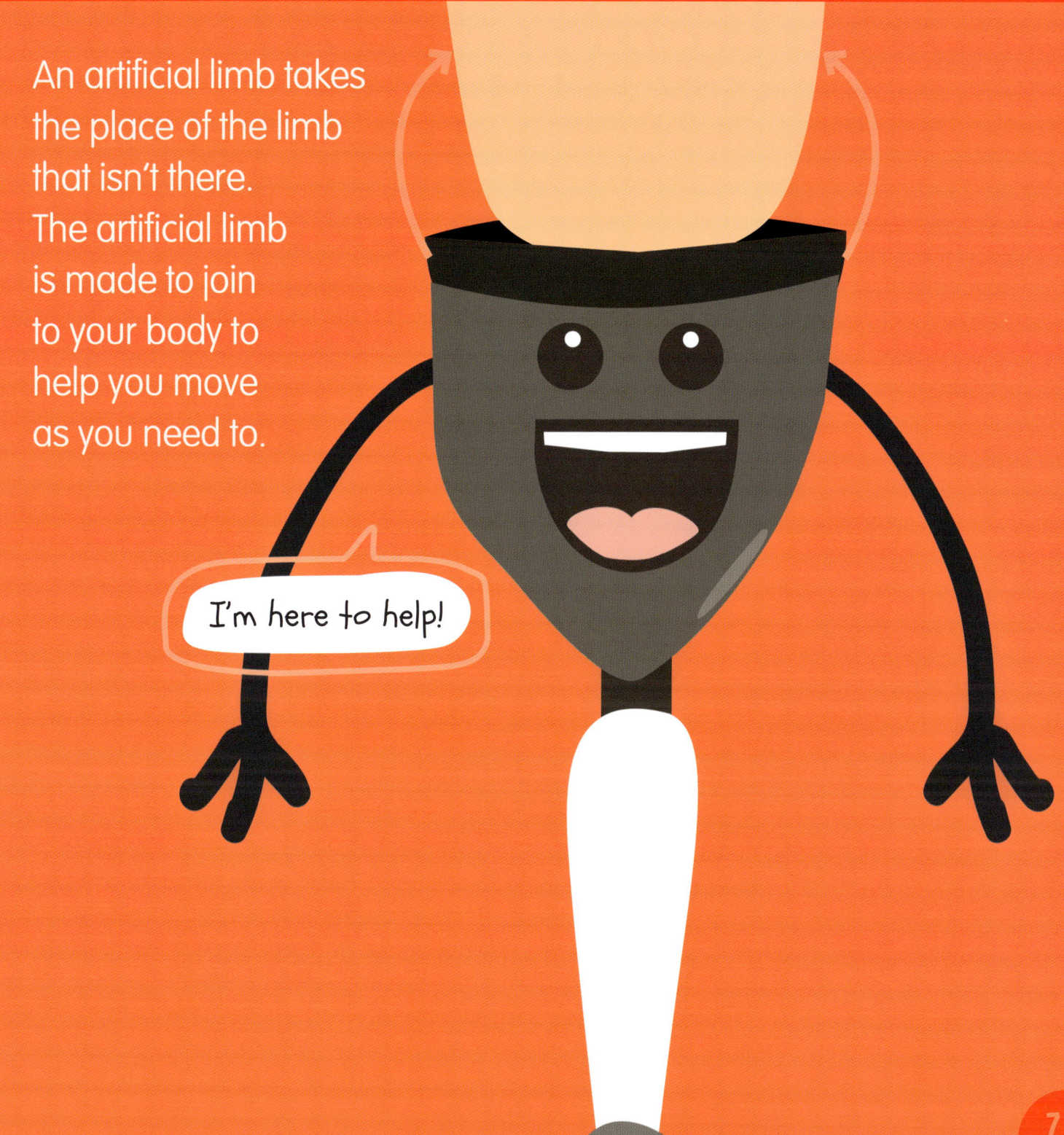

WHAT HAPPENS IF I NEED AN ARTIFICIAL LIMB?

If you've had an operation to remove a limb, you'll need to stay in hospital for several days. You'll be given medicine to make sure you're not in pain.

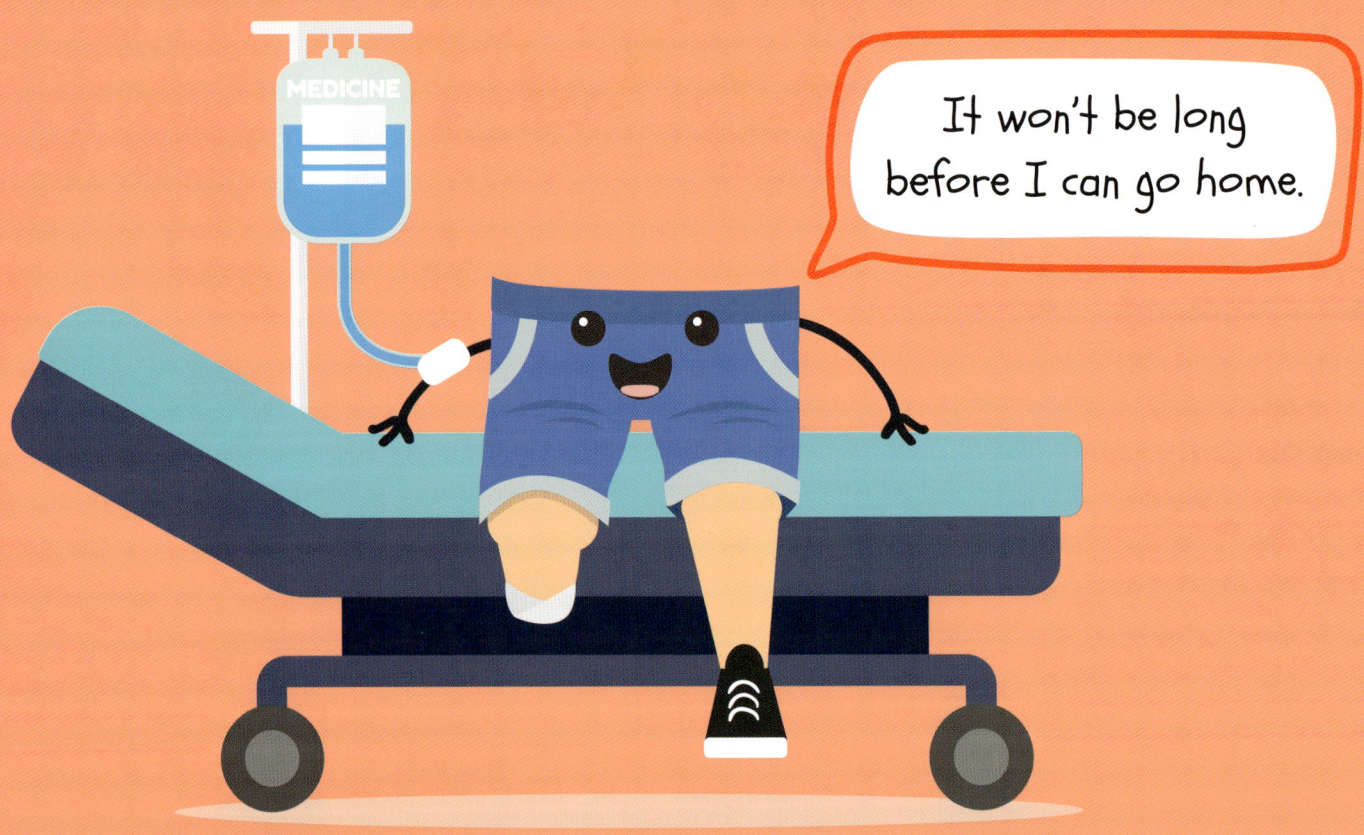

It won't be long before I can go home.

The area where your body part was removed is known as your stump. You will have to visit your doctor a lot to check on your stump and get ready for your new artificial limb.

You'll need to make sure you take good care of your stump. Make sure you wash the skin on your stump at least once each day. You'll need to check it for signs of **infection**, too.

The doctors will tell you how to take care of me.

Your stump might be sore to touch. The doctors will show you things you can do to help with this. You might need to rub or tap the end of your stump every day.

Make sure you are gentle when touching your stump.

You might be given a type of stocking to put over your stump to get it in the right shape for your artificial limb.

You might be told to keep your stump in the right position. Your doctors will tell you exactly what you need to do.

GETTING AN ARTIFICIAL LIMB

If you are able to have an artificial limb, you may need to do some exercises to make sure your body is ready to start using a new limb.

I'll need a bit of extra care before you get your artificial limb, too.

Your artificial limb will be made to fit your stump. You will need to go for different **appointments** to try out your new limb and learn how to use it.

WEARING YOUR ARTIFICIAL LIMB

There are different types of artificial limb and the doctor will decide which one is best suited to your needs. The person who fits your artificial limb is called a prosthetist.

PROSTHETIC LIMB

Your artificial limb is also known as a prosthetic limb.

Some artificial limbs can be used as you would have used your body part. Other types of artificial limb are used to look like the body part rather than work like it.

Your artificial limb will be made of **materials** that are light but strong. This helps you to move more easily. The artificial limb will have a socket into which you put your stump.

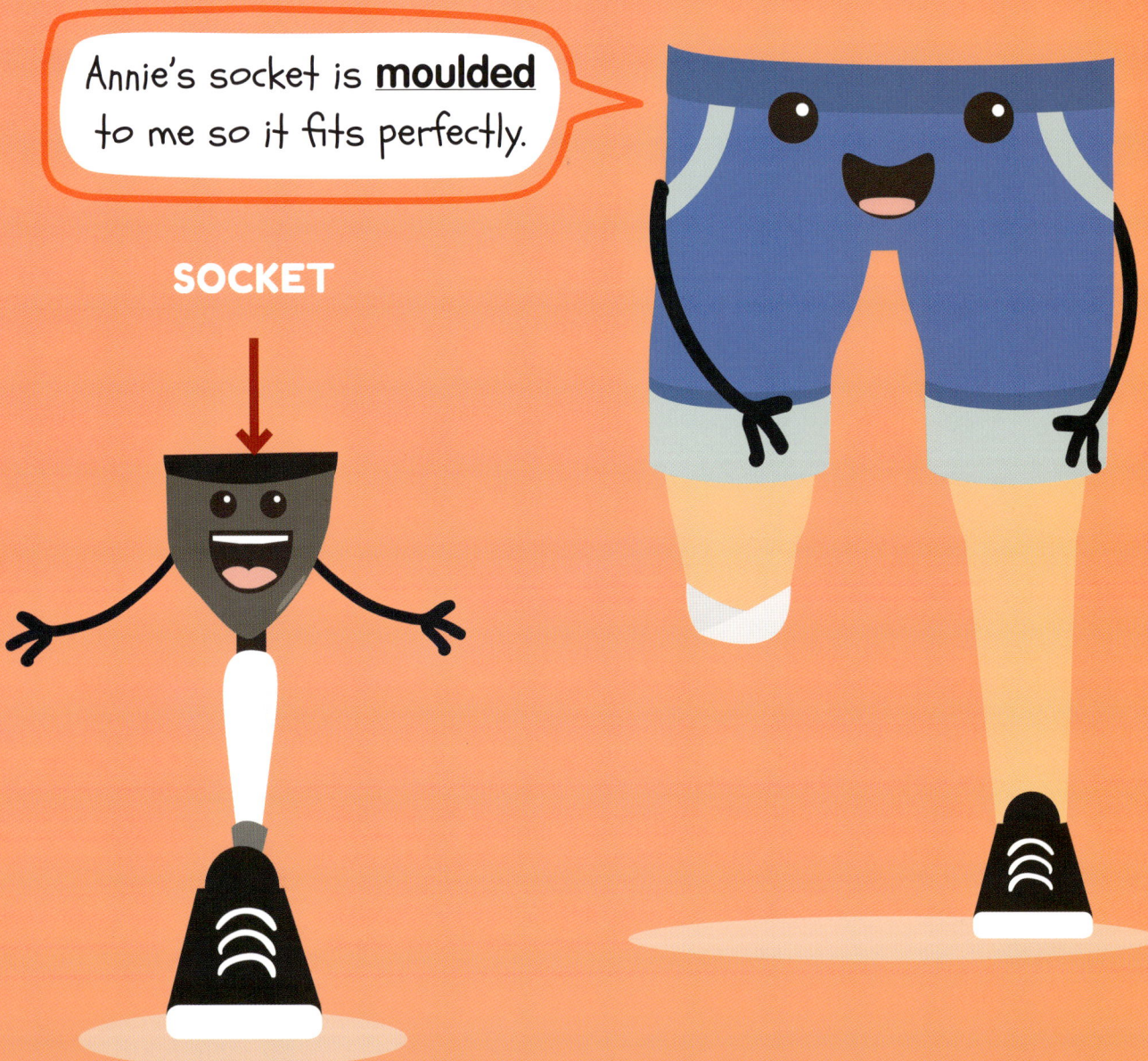

You might find that your artificial limb will need to be **repaired** after you have been using it for a while. You may also need to have it **adjusted** if your stump changes size.

DOS AND DON'TS

DON'T forget that not all artificial limbs are waterproof, so yours may need to be taken off when you swim, shower or bath.

DO try to eat healthily.

DO be patient when learning to use your artificial limb. It can take some time to get used to it.

It won't take long before you're used to me, Lee-Lee.

DON'T forget to check your stump to make sure it looks as it should.

LIFE WITH YOUR ARTIFICIAL LIMB

You will have your stump for the rest of your life, but you might not always wear your artificial limb. You may find that you begin to learn new ways of doing everyday activities.

I'm here whenever you need me, Lee-Lee.

If you find that wearing your artificial limb all the time is too tiring, you could take a break sometimes. If you have an artificial leg, you could use crutches or a wheelchair instead.

GLOSSARY

ADJUSTED   moved or changed
APPOINTMENTS   meetings with someone at particular times
ARTIFICIAL   made by humans and not natural
INFECTION   the result of being affected by a disease
MATERIALS   things from which objects are made
MOULDED   shaped
OPERATION   something done to a body to remove or mend something
REMOVED   taken away
REPAIRED   fixed or mended

INDEX

BODY 7, 9, 14, 17
DOCTORS 9, 10, 11, 13, 16, 19
EXERCISES 14
HOSPITALS 8
MEDICINE 8
MOVING 7, 18
PAIN 8
PROSTHETISTS 16
SKIN 10
SOCKETS 18
STUMPS 9–3, 15, 18–19, 21–22
WASH 10